Python Mini Manual
CodeCraft Dynamics

Chapter 1: Introduction

Overview of Python and its Evolution

Python is a high-level, interpreted, and general-purpose programming language that was first released in 1991 by Guido van Rossum. It was designed with a focus on code readability, making it easy to learn and use for both beginners and experienced programmers. Python's simple yet powerful syntax, combined with its versatility and extensive standard library, has made it one of the most popular and widely-used programming languages in the world.

A Brief History of Python

Python's origins can be traced back to the late 1980s when Guido van Rossum, a Dutch programmer working at the National Research Institute for Mathematics and Computer Science (CWI) in the Netherlands, was in search of a hobby programming project. He wanted to create a language that would be easy to read and write, and would cater to the needs of both programmers and end-users.

Van Rossum drew inspiration from several programming languages, including ABC, Modula-3, and even the Unix scripting language, Perl. The name "Python" was derived from the surreal comedy troupe Monty Python, which van Rossum was a fan of.

In February 1991, van Rossum published the first public version of Python, version 0.9.0, on the alt.sources Usenet newsgroup. The language quickly gained popularity among programmers, and by 1994, Python had reached version 1.0, marking its official release.

Over the years, Python has undergone several major revisions, with each new version introducing new features, improvements, and bug fixes. Some of the most significant milestones in Python's evolution include:

1. **Python 2.0** (2000): This version introduced significant enhancements, including support for Unicode, garbage collection, and list comprehensions.
2. **Python 2.4** (2004): This release added generator expressions, decorators, and the built-in sum() and enumerate() functions.
3. **Python 3.0** (2008): Python 3 marked a major overhaul of the language, introducing several backward-incompatible changes and improvements, such as better Unicode support, a new I/O system, and a stricter separation of binary and text

data.

4. **Python 3.5** (2015): This version introduced several new features, including type annotations, the @ operator for matrix multiplication, and the async and await keywords for asynchronous programming.

5. **Python 3.7** (2018): Python 3.7 introduced several new language features, such as postponed evaluation of annotations, the __future__ module, and the dataclasses module.

6. **Python 3.8** (2019): This release introduced assignment expressions (the walrus operator :=), positional-only parameters, and the math module gained support for additional mathematical constants and functions.

7. **Python 3.9** (2020): Python 3.9 introduced several new features, including the zoneinfo module for working with time zones, the graphlib module for creating flat and hierarchical graphs, and the ability to use type annotations in more places.

8. **Python 3.10** (2021): This version introduced several new features and improvements, including structural pattern matching, the match statement, and the ability to use parenthesized context managers with a with statement.

9. **Python 3.11** (2022): Python 3.11 introduced several new features and improvements, including the tomllib module for working with TOML files, the typing.TypeAlias feature for creating type aliases, and improved error messages for type annotations.

Over the years, Python has grown from a small scripting language to a powerful and versatile programming language used in a wide range of applications, from web development and scientific computing to data analysis, machine learning, and artificial intelligence.

Python's Philosophy and Design Principles

Python's design and development are guided by a set of principles known as the "Zen of Python." These principles, which can be accessed by running the import this command in the Python interpreter, emphasize simplicity, readability, and pragmatism. The Zen of Python serves as a guide for both the language's development and the coding practices of Python programmers.

Some of the key principles of the Zen of Python include:

- **Beautiful is better than ugly**: Python code should be clean, readable, and aesthetically pleasing.
- **Explicit is better than implicit**: Python code should be explicit and self-documenting, avoiding unnecessary obscurity or ambiguity.
- **Simple is better than complex**: Python favors simple solutions over complex ones, making the language easy to learn and use.
- **Flat is better than nested**: Python encourages flat structures and discourages excessive nesting, which can make code harder to read and maintain.
- **Readability counts**: Python emphasizes code readability, as it is often easier to read and understand code than to write it from scratch.
- **There should be one—and preferably only one—obvious way to do it**: Python aims to have a single, consistent way of accomplishing a task, reducing the potential for confusion and errors.
- **If the implementation is hard to explain, it's a bad idea**: Python favors solutions that are easy to understand and

explain, making it easier to maintain and collaborate on code.

- **Namespaces are one honking great idea—let's do more of those!**: Python's use of namespaces helps to organize code and avoid naming conflicts.

These principles have helped shape Python into a language that prioritizes simplicity, clarity, and readability, making it accessible to a wide range of users, from beginners to experienced developers.

Python Community and Ecosystem

One of Python's greatest strengths lies in its vibrant and active community. Python has a large and diverse user base, spanning various industries and domains, from web development and scientific computing to data analysis, machine learning, and artificial intelligence.

The Python Software Foundation

The Python Software Foundation (PSF) is a non-profit organization that holds the intellectual property rights to the Python programming language and manages its development and distribution. The PSF was founded in 2001 and is dedicated to promoting, protecting, and advancing the Python programming language and its community.

The PSF is responsible for several key initiatives, including:

- Managing and maintaining the official Python distributions and releases
- Organizing and sponsoring various Python conferences and events
- Providing grants and funding for Python-related projects and initiatives
- Promoting the use of Python in education and research
- Supporting and encouraging diversity and inclusivity within the Python community

The PSF is governed by a board of directors and relies on the contributions and support of volunteers from the Python community.

Python Community Resources

The Python community offers a wealth of resources for learning, collaborating, and staying up-to-date with the latest developments in the language and its ecosystem. Some of the most popular resources include:

1. **Python.org**: The official website for Python, maintained by the Python Software Foundation. It provides a wealth of information, including documentation, downloads, news, and resources for learning and contributing to Python.
2. **Python Package Index (PyPI)**: PyPI is the official repository for third-party Python packages and libraries. It hosts thousands of packages that can be easily installed and used in Python projects, vastly extending the language's capabilities.
3. **Python Mailing Lists**: The Python community maintains several mailing lists for discussions, announcements, and support related to various Python topics. These include python-list (general discussion), python-dev (core development), and various topical mailing lists.
4. **Python Conferences and Meetups**: Python has a thriving community of local and international conferences, meetups, and user groups. These events provide opportunities for networking, learning, and collaborating with other Python enthusiasts and professionals.
5. **Online Communities and Forums**: Python has a strong presence on various online communities and forums, such as Reddit's r/Python, Stack Overflow, and dedicated Python forums like Python Forum and Discourse Python.
6. **Python Books and Tutorials**: There is a wealth of books, tutorials, and online resources available for learning Python

and exploring its various applications and libraries. These range from beginner-friendly introductions to advanced topics like web development, data science, and machine learning.

7. **Python Blogs and Podcasts**: Many Python developers and enthusiasts maintain blogs and podcasts, sharing their experiences, insights, and tutorials on various Python-related topics.

8. **Open-Source Projects**: Python has a vast ecosystem of open-source projects hosted on platforms like GitHub, GitLab, and Bitbucket. Contributing to or using these projects is an excellent way to learn, collaborate, and contribute to the Python community.

This strong and vibrant community is one of Python's greatest assets, providing support, resources, and opportunities for collaboration and growth to developers of all skill levels.

Python's Versatility and Applications

Python's versatility and ease of use have made it a popular choice for a wide range of applications across various domains. Some of the major areas where Python is widely used include:

1. **Web Development**: Python has several powerful web frameworks, such as Django, Flask, and Pyramid, which make it an excellent choice for building web applications, APIs, and microservices.

2. **Scientific Computing and Data Analysis**: Python's rich ecosystem of scientific computing libraries, such as NumPy, SciPy, Pandas, and Matplotlib, has made it a go-to language for data analysis, numerical computing, and scientific research.

3. **Machine Learning and Artificial Intelligence**: Python's libraries like TensorFlow, PyTorch, Scikit-learn, and Keras have made it a popular choice for developing and deploying machine learning and artificial intelligence models.

4. **Automation and Scripting**: Python's simplicity and cross-platform compatibility make it an ideal choice for automating tasks, writing scripts, and developing system administration tools.

5. **Game Development**: With libraries like Pygame, Panda3D, and PyOpenGL, Python can be used for creating games and multimedia applications.

6. **Education and Academia**: Python's readability and simplicity make it an excellent choice for teaching programming concepts in schools and universities.

7. **Finance and Trading**: Python's robust data analysis capabilities and integration with financial APIs have made it

popular in the finance industry for tasks such as algorithmic trading, risk analysis, and portfolio management.

8. **Internet of Things (IoT)**: Python's versatility and support for various hardware platforms make it a suitable choice for developing IoT applications and embedded systems.

9. **Network Programming**: Python's standard library and third-party libraries like Twisted and Scapy provide powerful tools for network programming, including web scraping, network scanning, and building network applications.

10. **DevOps and System Administration**: Python's ability to interact with operating systems and its vast library ecosystem make it a valuable tool for DevOps tasks, such as configuration management, automation, and system monitoring.

This versatility, combined with Python's ease of use and vibrant community, has contributed to its widespread adoption across various industries and domains.

Looking Ahead

As Python continues to evolve and grow, it remains a powerful and versatile language that is well-suited for a wide range of applications. With its strong emphasis on simplicity, readability, and community, Python is poised to maintain its position as one of the most popular and widely-used programming languages in the world.

In the upcoming chapters, we will dive deeper into the language's syntax, features, and ecosystem, exploring topics such as data types, control structures, functions, object-oriented programming, file I/O, and more. We will also cover best practices, tips, and techniques for writing efficient, maintainable, and idiomatic Python code.

Whether you are a beginner just starting your journey with Python or an experienced developer looking to expand your knowledge and skills, this book aims to provide a comprehensive and practical guide to the Python programming language.

Chapter 2: Python Basics

This chapter will introduce you to the fundamentals of working with Python, including installation, running Python code, and using the interactive interpreter. We'll also cover some basic syntax and concepts that will lay the foundation for your Python programming journey.

Installation and Setup

Before you can start writing and running Python code, you'll need to have Python installed on your system. Python is available for various operating systems, including Windows, macOS, and Linux.

Installing Python

There are several ways to install Python on your system, depending on your operating system and preferences. Here are the most common methods:

1. **Official Python Distribution**: You can download the latest version of Python from the official Python website (https://www.python.org/downloads/). The website provides installers for Windows, macOS, and various Linux distributions.

2. **Package Managers**: Many operating systems include Python in their package repositories, making it easy to install using the system's package manager. For example, on Ubuntu or other Debian-based Linux distributions, you can install Python using the apt package manager:

```
sudo apt-get update
sudo apt-get install python3
```
On macOS, you can use the Homebrew package manager:
```
brew install python3
```

1. **Integrated Development Environments (IDEs)**: Some IDEs, such as PyCharm, Visual Studio Code, and Spyder, come bundled with Python or provide an option to install Python during the IDE setup process.

2. **Virtualization and Containerization**: If you prefer to keep your development environment isolated, you can use virtualization tools like VirtualBox or containerization solutions like Docker to set up a Python environment.

3. **Anaconda Distribution**: For scientific computing and data

science applications, the Anaconda distribution (https://www.anaconda.com/distribution/) is a popular choice. It comes with Python and a vast collection of pre-installed scientific computing packages.

Regardless of the installation method you choose, it's generally recommended to install the latest stable version of Python 3.x. Python 2.x is no longer actively developed and reached its end-of-life in 2020.

Setting up the Environment (Optional)

While not strictly necessary, setting up a dedicated development environment can be beneficial, especially for larger projects or when working with multiple Python versions or dependencies. Here are a few options:

1. **Virtual Environments**: Python's built-in venv module allows you to create isolated Python environments, separate from your system's global Python installation. This is useful for managing dependencies and avoiding conflicts between projects.
2. **Conda Environments**: If you're using the Anaconda distribution, you can create and manage environments using the conda package and environment management system.
3. **Python Distributions and IDEs**: Many Python distributions and IDEs, such as Anaconda and PyCharm, provide tools for creating and managing environments out of the box.
4. **Docker Containers**: You can create and manage Python environments using Docker containers, which provide a consistent and reproducible environment across different systems.

Setting up a dedicated development environment is optional for small projects or when you're just starting with Python, but it's generally recommended as your projects grow in complexity and have more dependencies.

Interactive Interpreter Usage

One of Python's strengths is its interactive interpreter, which allows you to execute Python code interactively and explore the language's features. The interactive interpreter is a great tool for learning, experimenting, and testing small code snippets.

Starting the Interactive Interpreter

To start the interactive interpreter, open a terminal or command prompt and type python (or python3 if you have multiple Python versions installed). You should see the Python version information and the interpreter prompt (>>>):

```
$ python3
Python 3.9.1 (default, Dec 11 2020, 16:51:43)
[GCC 10.2.1 20201203 (Red Hat 10.2.1-9)] on linux
Type "help", "copyright", "credits" or "license" for more information.
>>>
```

You can now start typing Python code at the prompt, and it will be executed immediately.

Basic Arithmetic and Expressions

The interactive interpreter is great for performing basic arithmetic operations and evaluating expressions. Here are a few examples:

```
>>> 2 + 3
5
>>> 10 * 4
40
>>> 15 / 3
5.0
>>> 2 ** 4 # Exponentiation
16
>>> (2 + 3) * 4 # Parentheses for precedence
20
```

You can also use the interactive interpreter to work with strings, lists, and other data types:

```
>>> name = "Alice"
>>> print(f"Hello, {name}!")
Hello, Alice!
>>> fruits = ["apple", "banana", "orange"]
>>> fruits[1]
'banana'
```

Exploring Built-in Functions and Modules

The interactive interpreter is also useful for exploring Python's built-in functions and modules. You can import modules and call their functions directly:

```
>>> import math
>>> math.sqrt(16)
4.0
>>> math.pi
```

```
3.141592653589793
```

You can also access the built-in help() function to get documentation on Python's built-in modules, functions, and data types:

```
>>> help(math)
Help on module math:
NAME
math

...
```

Executing Code from Files

While the interactive interpreter is great for exploration and testing, you'll eventually need to write and execute Python code in files. To execute a Python script, save your code in a file with a .py extension (e.g., script.py), and then run the file using the python command:

```
$ python script.py
```

Alternatively, you can use an Integrated Development Environment (IDE) or a text editor with Python support, which often provides features like code completion, debugging, and project management.

Writing and Running Python Scripts

Now that you've learned how to use the interactive interpreter, let's explore how to write and run Python scripts in files.

Python Script Files

Python scripts are simply text files containing Python code. By convention, Python script files use the .py extension, but this is not strictly necessary. Python files can be created and edited using any text editor or an IDE with Python support.

Here's an example of a simple Python script (hello.py) that prints a greeting:

```
# hello.py
name = input("What is your name? ")
print(f"Hello, {name}!")
```

To run this script, save the file and execute it using the python command:

```
$ python hello.py
What is your name? Alice
Hello, Alice!
```

Python Modules and Importing

In Python, you can organize your code into reusable modules. A module is simply a Python file that contains definitions (functions, classes, variables, etc.) that can be imported and used in other Python scripts or modules.

Here's an example of a simple module (greetings.py) that defines a function to greet someone:

```
# greetings.py
def greet(name):
print(f"Hello, {name}!")
```

You can import this module in another Python script (main.py) and use the greet() function:

```
# main.py
import greetings
name = input("What is your name? ")
greetings.greet(name)
```

When you run main.py, it will use the greet() function defined in the greetings module:

```
$ python main.py
What is your name? Alice
Hello, Alice!
```

Python's module system allows you to organize your code into logical units, promote code reuse, and manage dependencies between different parts of your application.

Python Package Structure

As your Python projects grow in complexity, you may want to organize your code into packages. A package is a collection of Python modules organized in a directory hierarchy.

Here's an example of a simple package structure:

```
mypackage/
__init__.py
module1.py
module2.py
subpackage/
__init__.py
module3.py
```

The __init__.py files are special files that mark the directories as Python packages. They can also contain initialization code or define variables and functions that can be imported from the package.

To import modules or subpackages from this package structure, you would use the following syntax:

```
import mypackage.module1
import mypackage.subpackage.module3
```

This hierarchical package structure helps to organize your code, avoid naming conflicts, and make your project more maintainable as it grows in size and complexity.

Python Script Arguments

Python scripts can also accept command-line arguments, allowing you to pass parameters or options when running the script. You can access these arguments using the sys.argv list from the sys module.

Here's an example script (greet_with_args.py) that greets a person using a command-line argument:

```
# greet_with_args.py
import sys
```

```python
if len(sys.argv) < 2:
print("Usage: python greet_with_args.py <name>")
sys.exit(1)
name = sys.argv[1]
print(f"Hello, {name}!")
```

To run this script, you provide the name as a command-line argument:

```
$ python greet_with_args.py Alice
Hello, Alice!
```

If you run the script without providing a name argument, it will display a usage message and exit:

```
$ python greet_with_args.py
Usage: python greet_with_args.py <name>
```

Working with command-line arguments can be useful when you need to pass configuration options, file paths, or other input data to your Python scripts.

Python Shebang Line (Unix/Linux)

On Unix-like systems (e.g., Linux, macOS), you can make Python scripts executable by adding a "shebang" line at the beginning of the script file. The shebang line specifies the interpreter that should be used to execute the script.

Here's an example of a Python script (script.py) with a shebang line:

```python
#!/usr/bin/env python3
# Your Python code goes here...
print("Hello, World!")
```

The first line #!/usr/bin/env python3 tells the system to use the python3 interpreter to execute the script. The env command is used to find the Python interpreter in the user's environment, making the script more portable across different Unix-like systems.

After adding the shebang line, you need to make the script executable using the chmod command:

$ chmod +x script.py

Now, you can run the script directly without specifying the python command:

$ ./script.py

Hello, World!

The shebang line is a Unix/Linux convention and is not used on Windows systems, where you would typically run Python scripts using the python command.

Chapter 3: Python Syntax Basics

In this chapter, we will explore the basic syntax and language features of Python. We will cover topics such as variables, data types, operators, control structures, functions, lambda expressions, and exception handling. By the end of this chapter, you should have a solid understanding of Python syntax and be able to write simple Python programs.

Variables

In Python, a variable is a named location used to store data in memory. It is helpful to think of variables as a container that holds data that can be changed later in the program. For example, you might create a variable called x and assign it the value of 10. In Python, you do not need to declare the variable type, it is dynamically inferred from the value you assign.

Here's an example of how to declare a variable in Python:

x = 10

In this example, x is the variable, and we have assigned it the integer value 10. You can also assign other types of values to variables, such as strings or floating-point numbers.

name = "Alice"

pi = 3.14159

In Python, variable names are case-sensitive, so name, Name, and NAME would each be different variables. Variable names can be as short as one letter or as long as you like, but they must begin with a letter or an underscore (_), and cannot start with a number.

Data Types

In Python, data types are an integral part of the language. They define the type of data that a variable can hold. Python has several built-in data types, including integers, floats, strings, and booleans.

1. **Integers**: Integers in Python are whole numbers that can be positive or negative. For example, 5, -10, and 0 are all integers.

```
x = 5
y = -10
z = 0
```

1. **Floats**: Floats, or floating-point numbers, are numbers that contain a decimal point. For example, 5.0, -10.2, and 0.0 are all floats.

```
x = 5.0
y = -10.2
z = 0.0
```

1. **Strings**: Strings in Python are sequences of characters. They are defined by enclosing characters in quotes. Python allows for both single and double quotes. For example, 'hello' and "world" are both strings.

```
x = 'hello'
y = "world"
```

1. **Booleans**: Booleans represent one of two values: True or False. In Python, boolean values are capitalized.

```
x = True
y = False
```

Operators

Operators are special symbols in Python that carry out arithmetic or logical computation. The value that the operator operates on is called the operand.

1. **Arithmetic Operators**: Arithmetic operators are used to perform mathematical operations like addition, subtraction, multiplication, etc.

```
x = 10
y = 5
# Addition
print(x + y) # Output: 15
# Subtraction
print(x - y) # Output: 5
# Multiplication
print(x * y) # Output: 50
# Division
print(x / y) # Output: 2.0
```

1. **Comparison Operators**: Comparison operators are used to compare values. It returns either True or False according to the condition.

```
x = 10
y = 5
# Greater than
print(x > y) # Output: True
# Less than
print(x < y) # Output: False
```

```python
# Equal to
print(x == y) # Output: False
```

1. **Logical Operators**: Logical operators are and, or, and not operators.

```python
x = True
y = False
# Output: True
print(x and y)
# Output: False
print(x or y)
# Output: False
print(not x)
```

1. **Assignment Operators**: Assignment operators are used in Python to assign values to variables.

```python
x = 10
x += 5 # Add AND: is equivalent to x = x + 5
print(x) # Output: 15
```

Control Structures

Control structures in Python are used to control the flow of execution of the program based on certain conditions or loops. They include if statements, loops (for and while), and break and continue statements.

1. **If Statements**: If statements are used for decision-making operations. It contains a body of code which is executed when the condition provided in the if statement is True.

```
x = 10
if x > 5:
print("x is greater than 5")
```

1. **Loops**: In Python, for and while loops are used for iterative tasks. The for loop is used to iterate over a sequence (like a list, tuple, dictionary, set, or string) or other iterable objects. Iterating over a sequence is called traversal.

```
# Using for loop
for i in range(5):
print(i)
# Using while loop
i = 0
while i < 5:
print(i)
i += 1
```

1. **Break and Continue Statements**: The break statement terminates the loop in which it is present. After that, the control will move to the statements that are present after the loop. If the break statement is inside a nested loop, then it

will terminate only those loops which contains break statement. The continue statement is used to skip the rest of the code inside the enclosing loop for the current iteration only. The loop does not terminate but continues with the next iteration.

```python
# Using break
for i in range(5):
if i == 3:
break
print(i)
# Using continue
for i in range(5):
if i == 3:
continue
print(i)
```

Functions

Functions are reusable blocks of code that perform a specific task. They help to modularize and organize your code, making it more readable and maintainable.

Defining Functions

In Python, you can define a function using the def keyword, followed by the function name, parentheses for the parameters, and a colon. The function body is indented and can contain any number of statements.

Here's a simple example of a function that adds two numbers:

```
def add_numbers(x, y):
    """

    Adds two numbers and returns the result.
    """

    result = x + y
    return result
# Calling the function
sum = add_numbers(3, 5)
print(sum) # Output: 8
```

In this example, add_numbers is the function name, and x and y are the parameters. The docstring (triple-quoted string) provides a brief description of the function's purpose.

The return statement is used to return a value from the function. If no return statement is present, the function returns None by default.

Function Parameters

Python functions can accept different types of parameters:

1. **Positional Parameters**: These are the basic parameters that are passed to the function in the same order as they are defined.

```
def greet(name, age):
print(f"Hello, {name}! You are {age} years old.")
greet("Alice", 25) # Output: Hello, Alice! You are 25 years old.
```

1. **Default Parameters**: You can provide default values for parameters, which are used if no value is supplied when calling the function.

```
def greet(name, greeting="Hello"):
print(f"{greeting}, {name}!")
greet("Bob") # Output: Hello, Bob!
greet("Alice", "Hi") # Output: Hi, Alice!
```

1. **Keyword Arguments**: You can pass parameters using keyword arguments, allowing you to specify the parameter names explicitly.

```
def greet(name, age, city="New York"):
print(f"Hello, {name}! You are {age} years old and live in {city}.")
greet("Bob", 30, city="Los Angeles") # Output: Hello, Bob! You are 30 years old and live in Los Angeles.
greet("Alice", age=25, city="Paris") # Output: Hello, Alice! You are 25 years old and live in Paris.
```

1. **Arbitrary Arguments (*args)**: You can use the *args syntax

to pass an arbitrary number of positional arguments as a tuple.

```python
def sum_numbers(*args):
total = 0
for num in args:
total += num
return total
print(sum_numbers(1, 2, 3)) # Output: 6
print(sum_numbers(4, 5)) # Output: 9
```

1. **Arbitrary Keyword Arguments (**kwargs)**: You can use the **kwargs syntax to pass an arbitrary number of keyword arguments as a dictionary.

```python
def print_info(**kwargs):
for key, value in kwargs.items():
print(f"{key}: {value}")
print_info(name="Alice", age=25, city="New York")
```

These different parameter types provide flexibility in how you define and call functions, allowing you to write more versatile and reusable code.

Lambda Functions

Python also supports anonymous functions, known as lambda functions. Lambda functions are small, one-line functions that can be defined without a name. They are typically used in situations where you need a simple function for a short period of time, such as when passing a function as an argument to another function or when working with functional programming constructs like map, filter, and reduce.

Here's an example of a lambda function that squares a number:

square = lambda x: x ** 2

print(square(3)) *# Output: 9*

In this example, lambda x: x ** 2 defines an anonymous function that takes one argument x and returns its square. The function is assigned to the variable square, which can then be used like a regular function.

Lambda functions are limited to a single expression and cannot contain statements or multiple lines of code. However, they can be useful for writing concise and readable code in certain situations.

Function Scope and Closures

In Python, variables have different scopes depending on where they are defined. There are two main types of scope: global scope and local scope.

1. **Global Scope**: Variables defined outside of any function or class are considered global and can be accessed from anywhere in the code.
2. **Local Scope**: Variables defined inside a function are considered local and can only be accessed within that function.

Here's an example that illustrates the difference between global and local scope:

```python
# Global variable
x = 10
def my_function():
# Local variable
y = 20
print(x) # Accessing global variable
print(y) # Accessing local variable
my_function() # Output: 10, 20
print(x) # Output: 10
print(y) # Error: NameError: name 'y' is not defined
```

In this example, x is a global variable, while y is a local variable defined inside the my_function function. The function can access both the global variable x and the local variable y. However, trying to access the local variable y outside the function results in a NameError.

Python also supports nested functions and closures, which allow inner functions to access variables from the outer function's scope, even after the outer function has finished executing.

```python
def outer_function(x):
y = 10
def inner_function(z):
# inner_function can access x and y
return x + y + z
return inner_function
closure = outer_function(5)
print(closure(3)) # Output: 18
```

In this example, inner_function is a closure that captures the variables x and y from the outer_function scope. Even after outer_function has finished executing, inner_function (assigned to the closure variable) can still access and use the values of x and y.

Closures are powerful constructs in Python that enable functions to maintain state and provide a way to implement functional programming patterns like currying and partial function application.

Exception Handling

In any non-trivial program, errors and exceptional situations are bound to occur. These could be caused by various factors, such as invalid user input, network failures, or issues with external resources like files or databases. When such exceptions occur, they can cause your program to terminate abruptly or behave unexpectedly. Exception handling is a way to gracefully handle these exceptional situations and prevent your program from crashing.

What are Exceptions?

In Python, an exception is an error that occurs during the execution of a program. When an exception is raised, it disrupts the normal flow of the program's instructions. If left unhandled, exceptions can lead to program termination and potentially corrupt data or leave resources in an inconsistent state.

Exceptions in Python are represented as objects that are instances of classes derived from the base Exception class. Some common built-in exceptions include ValueError, TypeError, ZeroDivisionError, FileNotFoundError, and many others.

Why is Exception Handling Important?

Exception handling is crucial for several reasons:

1. **Robustness**: By anticipating and handling potential exceptions, you can make your program more robust and less prone to crashing or behaving unexpectedly.
2. **Error Reporting**: Exception handling allows you to provide informative error messages to users or log errors for debugging purposes, making it easier to identify and fix issues.
3. **Resource Management**: Exceptions can occur during resource acquisition or usage (e.g., opening files, network connections), and proper exception handling ensures that resources are cleaned up properly, even in the event of an error.
4. **Control Flow**: Exception handling can be used to implement alternative control flows or fallback mechanisms when certain conditions are met or specific errors occur.

Try, Except, Finally, and Raise Statements

Python provides several statements for handling exceptions:

1. **try**: The try statement is used to enclose the code that might raise an exception. If an exception occurs within the try block, it is caught and handled by the corresponding except block.

```
try:
# Code that might raise an exception
result = x / y
except ZeroDivisionError:
# Handle the exception
print("Error: Division by zero")
```

1. **except**: The except block is used to catch and handle specific types of exceptions. You can have multiple except blocks to handle different types of exceptions.

```
try:
# Code that might raise an exception
file = open("non_existent_file.txt", "r")
except FileNotFoundError:
# Handle the FileNotFoundError exception
print("Error: File not found")
except PermissionError:
# Handle the PermissionError exception
print("Error: You don't have permission to access the file")
```

You can also catch multiple exception types in a single except block by providing a tuple of exception classes.

```python
try:
# Code that might raise an exception
...
except (ValueError, TypeError):
# Handle ValueError or TypeError exceptions
...
```

1. **else**: The optional else clause is executed if no exceptions are raised in the corresponding try block. This can be useful for separating the exception handling code from the code that should run when no exceptions occur.

```python
try:
# Code that might raise an exception
result = x / y
except ZeroDivisionError:
# Handle the exception
print("Error: Division by zero")
else:
# Code to run if no exceptions were raised
print(f"Result: {result}")
```

1. **finally**: The finally block is executed regardless of whether an exception was raised or not. This is typically used for cleanup code, such as closing files or releasing resources.

```python
try:
# Code that might raise an exception
file = open("data.txt", "r")
data = file.read()
except FileNotFoundError:
# Handle the exception
print("Error: File not found")
```

```
finally:
# Cleanup code
file.close()
```

1. **raise**: The raise statement is used to manually raise an exception. This can be useful for creating custom exceptions or propagating exceptions further up the call stack.

```
def validate_age(age):
if age < 0:
raise ValueError("Age cannot be negative")
# Other validation logic...
try:
age = int(input("Enter your age: "))
validate_age(age)
except ValueError as e:
print(e)
```

In this example, the validate_age function raises a ValueError if the age is negative. If this exception is raised and not caught within the function, it will propagate up to the try block where it can be handled.

Chapter 4: Built-in Types and Objects

Introduction

Python, as a dynamically typed language, offers a variety of built-in types and objects. These are the fundamental building blocks of data that we use to construct our programs. Understanding these types and how to use them is essential to programming in Python.

In Python, everything is an object, which means every entity has some metadata (called attributes) and associated functionality (called methods). These allow us to interact with the object and perform operations.

Built-in types in Python include the basic types like integers, floats, and strings, as well as collection types like lists, tuples, sets, and dictionaries. Python also provides several built-in functions that can operate on these types, such as len() to get the length of a collection, or int() to convert a value to an integer.

In this chapter, we will explore these built-in types and objects in more detail. We'll learn how to create and manipulate them, and understand their properties and methods. By the end of this chapter, you should have a solid understanding of Python's built-in types and how to work with them in your programs.

Numbers

Numbers in Python are an essential data type. They are immutable data types, meaning that changing the value of a number data type results in a newly allocated object. Python supports three types of numbers - integers, floating point numbers, and complex numbers.

1. **Integers**: Integers in Python can be of any length, they are only limited by the amount of memory available. Integers in Python can be represented in several bases (decimal, octal, hexadecimal, and binary).

```python
# Decimal
dec = 10
print(dec) # Output: 10
# Octal
oct = 0o12
print(oct) # Output: 10
# Hexadecimal
hex = 0xA
print(hex) # Output: 10
# Binary
bin = 0b1010
print(bin) # Output: 10
```

1. **Floating Point Numbers**: Floating point numbers in Python are notable because they have a decimal point in them, or use an exponential (e) to define the number.

```python
x = 10.5
y = 1.5e2
print(x) # Output: 10.5
```

```
print(y) # Output: 150.0
```

1. **Complex Numbers**: Complex numbers are written in the form, x + yj, where x is the real part and y is the imaginary part.

```
z = 2+3j
print(z) # Output: (2+3j)
```

Strings

Strings in Python are sequences of characters, enclosed in either single quotes (') or double quotes ("). Python treats single quotes the same as double quotes.

```
str1 = 'hello'
str2 = "world"
```

String Indexing: Python uses zero-based indexing. You can access individual characters using indexing and a range of characters using slicing.

```
str = 'hello'
print(str[0]) # Output: 'h'
print(str[1:3]) # Output: 'el'
```

String Methods: Python has a set of built-in methods that you can use on strings.

- upper(): Converts a string into upper case.
- lower(): Converts a string into lower case.
- split(): Splits the string at the specified separator and returns a list of strings.
- format(): Formats specified values in a string.

```
str = 'hello world'
print(str.upper()) # Output: 'HELLO WORLD'
print(str.lower()) # Output: 'hello world'
print(str.split()) # Output: ['hello', 'world']
print('Hello, {}'.format('World')) # Output: 'Hello, World'
```

Lists, Tuples, and Dictionaries

1. **Lists**: A list in Python is a collection of items which are ordered and changeable. Lists are written with square brackets [].

```
fruits = ['apple', 'banana', 'cherry']
print(fruits[0]) # Output: 'apple'
```

1. **Tuples**: A tuple in Python is a collection which is ordered and unchangeable. Tuples are written with round brackets ().

```
fruits = ('apple', 'banana', 'cherry')
print(fruits[0]) # Output: 'apple'
```

1. **Dictionaries**: A dictionary in Python is a collection which is unordered, changeable, and indexed. Dictionaries are written with curly brackets {}, and they have keys and values.

```
car = {
'brand': 'Ford',
'model': 'Mustang',
'year': 1964
}
print(car['brand']) # Output: 'Ford'
```

Sets and Frozensets

In Python, a set is an unordered collection of unique elements. Sets are mutable, meaning they can be changed after they are created. They are useful when the existence of an item in a collection is more important than the order or how many times it occurs.

Here's an example of how to create a set in Python:

fruits = {'apple', 'banana', 'cherry'}

A frozenset is a built-in set in Python that is immutable, meaning the elements of the set cannot be changed after it is assigned. While elements of a set can be modified at any time, elements of the frozenset remain the same after creation.

Here's an example of how to create a frozenset in Python:

fruits = frozenset(['apple', 'banana', 'cherry'])

Sets

A set in Python is an unordered collection of unique elements. Sets are mutable, meaning they can be changed after they are created. They are useful when the existence of an item in a collection is more important than the order or how many times it occurs.

Here's an example of how to create a set in Python:

```python
fruits = {'apple', 'banana', 'cherry'}
```

You can perform operations on sets like union, intersection, difference, and symmetric difference. Here are some examples:

```python
# Union of sets
A = {1, 2, 3}
B = {2, 3, 4}
print(A | B) # Output: {1, 2, 3, 4}
# Intersection of sets
print(A & B) # Output: {2, 3}
# Difference of sets
print(A - B) # Output: {1}
# Symmetric difference of sets
print(A ^ B) # Output: {1, 4}
```

You can also check if a set is a subset or superset of another set, and whether two sets are disjoint:

```python
# Check if A is a subset of B
print(A <= B) # Output: False
# Check if A is a superset of B
print(A >= B) # Output: False
# Check if A and B are disjoint sets
print(A.isdisjoint(B)) # Output: False
```

Frozensets

A frozenset in Python is a frozen set, which is an immutable version of a Python set object. While elements of a set can be modified at any time, elements of the frozenset remain the same after creation. This means you can use them as keys in a dictionary, unlike sets.

Here's an example of how to create a frozenset in Python:

fruits = frozenset(['apple', 'banana', 'cherry'])

Like sets, frozensets support methods like copy(), difference(), intersection(), isdisjoint(), issubset(), issuperset(), symmetric_difference(), and union(), but not add() or remove(), because frozensets are immutable.

Here are some examples:

A = frozenset([1, 2, 3])

B = frozenset([2, 3, 4])

Union of frozensets

print(A | B) # Output: frozenset({1, 2, 3, 4})

Intersection of frozensets

print(A & B) # Output: frozenset({2, 3})

Difference of frozensets

print(A - B) # Output: frozenset({1})

Symmetric difference of frozensets

print(A ^ B) # Output: frozenset({1, 4})

Chapter 5: File I/O and Streams

File I/O (Input/Output) operations are essential in most programming tasks, allowing you to read and write data from and to files. Python provides a comprehensive set of functions and methods for working with files and streams, making it easy to handle various types of data, including text and binary formats.

In this chapter, we'll explore the different aspects of file I/O and stream operations in Python, including reading and writing files, working with text and binary data, and utilizing standard I/O streams.

Reading and Writing Files

Python provides a built-in `open()` function to open files for reading or writing. This function returns a file object that represents the opened file and provides methods for interacting with its contents.

Opening a File

The `open()` function takes two arguments: the file path (either an absolute or relative path) and the mode in which the file should be opened. The mode specifies the purpose of the file operation, such as reading, writing, or appending data.

Here are some common file modes:

- `'r'` (read mode): Opens a file for reading. This is the default mode if none is specified.

- `'w'` (write mode): Opens a file for writing. If the file already exists, its contents will be truncated (deleted).

- `'a'` (append mode): Opens a file for appending data to the end of the file. If the file doesn't exist, it will be created.

- `'x'` (exclusive creation mode): Opens a file for exclusive creation, failing if the file already exists.

- `'b'` (binary mode): Opens a file in binary mode, allowing you to read and write binary data.

You can combine these modes as needed. For example, `'rb'` opens a file for reading binary data, and `'w+'` opens a file for both reading and writing, truncating the file if it already exists.

Here's an example of opening a file for reading:

file = open('example.txt', 'r')

It's important to close the file when you're done working with it to free up system resources. You can use the `close()` method or the `with` statement, which automatically closes the file when the block is exited:


```
# Using the close() method
    file = open('example.txt', 'r')
    # Do something with the file
```

```
file.close()
# Using the with statement (recommended)
with open('example.txt', 'r') as file:
# Do something with the file
pass # The file is automatically closed when the block ends
```

Reading from a File

Once you have a file object, you can read its contents using various methods. The `read()` method reads the entire file and returns its contents as a string:

    with open('example.txt', 'r') as file:
    content = file.read()
    print(content)

If you want to read the file line by line, you can use the `readlines()` method, which returns a list of strings, where each string represents a line from the file:

    with open('example.txt', 'r') as file:
    lines = file.readlines()
    for line in lines:
    print(line.rstrip()) # Remove the newline character

Alternatively, you can iterate over the file object directly, which reads one line at a time:

    with open('example.txt', 'r') as file:
    for line in file:
    print(line.rstrip())

Writing to a File

To write data to a file, you need to open it in write mode (``'w'``) or append mode (``'a''``). The `write()` method allows you to write a string to the file:

```python
with open('example.txt', 'w') as file:
file.write("This is a new line.\n')
file.write('And another line.\n')
```

If you want to write multiple lines at once, you can use the `writelines()` method, which takes an iterable (e.g., a list) of strings:

```python
lines = ['Line 1\n', 'Line 2\n', 'Line 3\n']
    with open('example.txt', 'w') as file:
    file.writelines(lines)
```

Working with Text and Binary Data

Python distinguishes between text and binary data when working with files. Text data is represented as strings, while binary data is represented as bytes objects.

Text Files

When you open a file in text mode (without the `"b"` flag), Python automatically handles the encoding and decoding of text data. By default, Python assumes the file is encoded in UTF-8, but you can specify a different encoding using the `encoding` parameter in the `open()` function:

```python
with open('example.txt', 'r', encoding='utf-8') as file:
content = file.read()
```

When writing to a text file, Python automatically encodes the string data according to the specified encoding.

Binary Files

Binary files are used to store non-text data, such as images, audio, video, or compressed data. When working with binary files, you should open them in binary mode by including the `'b'` flag in the mode string:

with open('example.bin', 'rb') as file:

binary_data = file.read()

In binary mode, the `read()` method returns a bytes object containing the raw binary data from the file. You can write binary data to a file using the `write()` method, passing a bytes object:

binary_data = b'some\xaa\xbb\xcc\xdd\xee'

with open('example.bin', 'wb') as file:

file.write(binary_data)

Standard I/O Streams

Python provides three standard I/O streams: `stdin` (standard input), `stdout` (standard output), and `stderr` (standard error). These streams allow you to read input from the user or write output to the console or a log file.

Standard Input (`stdin`)

The `stdin` stream is used to read user input from the console or a redirected input source. You can read data from `stdin` using the `input()` function or by accessing `sys.stdin` directly:

```python
user_input = input("Enter your name: ") # Reading from stdin
print(f"Hello, {user_input}!")
# Reading from sys.stdin
import sys
data = sys.stdin.readline()
print(f"You entered: {data}")
```

Standard Output (`stdout`)

The `stdout` stream is used to write output to the console or a redirected output destination. You can write to `stdout` using the `print()` function or by accessing `sys.stdout` directly:

```
print("Hello, world!") # Writing to stdout
# Writing to sys.stdout
import sys
sys.stdout.write("This is a message.\n")
```

Standard Error (`stderr`)

The `stderr` stream is used to write error or diagnostic messages to the console or a log file. It's commonly used for logging errors or warnings:

```python
import sys
try:
result = 10 / 0
except ZeroDivisionError as e:
sys.stderr.write(f"Error: {e}\n")
```

Redirecting Streams

You can redirect the standard I/O streams to files instead of the console or from one file to another. This is useful for logging or capturing output:

```python
# Redirecting stdout to a file
with open('output.txt', 'w') as file:
original_stdout = sys.stdout
sys.stdout = file
print("This message will be written to the file.")
sys.stdout = original_stdout
# Redirecting stdin from a file
with open('input.txt', 'r') as file:
original_stdin = sys.stdin
sys.stdin = file
data = input("Enter some data (from the file): ")
sys.stdin = original_stdin
print(f"You entered: {data}")
```

Chapter 6: Modules and Packages

In Python, you have the ability to organize your code into separate files called modules. Modules allow you to break down your program into smaller, more manageable pieces, making it easier to maintain and reuse code. Additionally, Python comes with a vast collection of built-in modules, known as the standard library, which provides a wide range of functionality to help you accomplish various tasks more efficiently.

You will learn about importing modules, creating and organizing your own packages, and exploring the Python standard library.

Importing Modules

Before you can use the functions, classes, or variables defined in a module, you need to import that module into your program. To import a module, you use the `import` statement followed by the name of the module.

For example, to import the `math` module, which provides mathematical functions and constants, you would write:

import math

After importing the module, you can access its contents using dot notation. For instance, to use the `pi` constant from the `math` module, you would write:

print(math.pi) # Output: 3.141592653589793

If you only need to use specific functions or variables from a module, you can import them directly using the `from` keyword. This can make your code more concise and easier to read.

from math import sqrt, pow

print(sqrt(16)) # Output: 4.0

print(pow(2, 3)) # Output: 8.0

In this example, we imported the `sqrt` and `pow` functions directly from the `math` module, allowing us to use them without the need for dot notation.

Creating and Organizing Packages

As your Python program grows larger, it becomes increasingly important to organize your code into separate modules and packages. A package is a collection of modules that can be imported and used together.

To create a package, you need to create a directory with an `__init__.py` file inside it. The `__init__.py` file serves as a marker, indicating to Python that the directory should be treated as a package. It can also be used to initialize the package and define code that should be executed when the package is imported.

Here's an example of a package structure:

```
mypackage/
__init__.py
module1.py
module2.py
subpackage/
__init__.py
module3.py
```

In this example, `mypackage` is the package, and it contains two modules (`module1.py` and `module2.py`) and a subpackage called `subpackage`. The `subpackage` also has an `__init__.py` file and a `module3.py` file.

To import a module from a package, you need to use dot notation, separating the package name, subpackage name (if applicable), and the module name with periods.

```
import mypackage.module1
import mypackage.subpackage.module3
```

Alternatively, you can import specific functions or classes directly from the modules:

```
from mypackage.module1 import my_function
from mypackage.subpackage.module3 import MyClass
```

By organizing your code into packages and modules, you can better structure your program, making it more maintainable and easier to share and distribute.

Exploring the Python Standard Library

Python comes with a vast and powerful standard library that provides a wide range of modules for various tasks, such as file handling, networking, data processing, and more. The standard library is an essential part of Python and is automatically available for use in your programs, without the need for any additional installations or configurations.

Here are some of the most commonly used modules from the Python standard library:

1. `os` module: This module provides a way to interact with the operating system, allowing you to perform tasks such as creating, deleting, or renaming files and directories, as well as executing system commands.

2. `sys` module: The `sys` module provides access to some variables and functions related to the Python interpreter and its environment. It allows you to work with command-line arguments, exit the program, and more.

3. `math` module: As mentioned earlier, the `math` module provides access to mathematical functions and constants, such as trigonometric functions, logarithmic functions, and values like `pi` and `e`.

4. `re` module: The `re` module allows you to work with regular expressions, which are powerful patterns used for searching, matching, and manipulating text.

5. `datetime` module: This module provides classes for working with dates, times, and time intervals, making it easier to perform date and time calculations and manipulations.

6. `random` module: The `random` module allows you to generate random numbers, make random choices, and perform other random operations, which can be useful in games, simulations, and other applications.

7. `json` module: The `json` module provides functions for encoding and decoding JSON (JavaScript Object Notation) data, which is a lightweight and human-readable data interchange format.

8. `csv` module: The `csv` module allows you to read and write CSV (Comma-Separated Values) files, which are commonly used for storing tabular data.

9. `urllib` module: The `urllib` module provides utilities for working with URLs, allowing you to retrieve data from web servers, handle HTTP requests and responses, and more.

10. `threading` and `multiprocessing` modules: These modules enable you to write concurrent programs that can take advantage of multiple processors or cores, improving performance and responsiveness.

These are just a few examples of the many modules available in the Python standard library. You can explore the full list of modules in the official Python documentation or by using the `help()` function in your Python interpreter or IDE.

```
import math

help(math) # Displays the documentation for the math module
```

By leveraging the power of the Python standard library, you can save time and effort by reusing existing code and functionality, rather than having to implement everything from scratch.

Chapter 7: Object-Oriented Programming (OOP)

Object-Oriented Programming (OOP) is a programming paradigm that revolves around the concept of objects, which are instances of classes. OOP provides a way to structure and organize code by combining data (attributes) and behavior (methods) into reusable and modular units called classes. This approach promotes code reusability, maintainability, and collaboration among developers.

Introduction

Object-Oriented Programming (OOP) is a programming paradigm that focuses on creating objects that contain both data and behavior. It is a way of organizing code that models real-world entities and their interactions. OOP is useful for several reasons:

Modularity: Code is organized into smaller, self-contained units (classes), making it easier to understand, maintain, and modify.

- Reusability: Once a class is created, it can be reused throughout the program or across multiple programs, saving time and effort.

- Encapsulation: Data and behavior are bundled together within objects, hiding implementation details and preventing direct access to internal components.

- Inheritance: New classes can inherit properties and behaviors from existing classes, promoting code reuse and enabling the creation of specialized versions of classes.

- Polymorphism: Objects of different classes can be treated as objects of a common superclass, allowing for flexibility and extensibility.

Classes and Objects

In Python, a class is a blueprint or a template for creating objects. It defines the properties (attributes) and behaviors (methods) that objects of that class will have. An object is an instance of a class, created from the blueprint defined by the class.

To define a class in Python, you use the `class` keyword followed by the name of the class:

```python
class Dog:
def __init__(self, name, breed):
self.name = name
self.breed = breed
def bark(self):
print(f"{self.name} says: Woof!")
```

In this example, we define a `Dog` class with an `__init__` method (a special method called a constructor) that initializes the `name` and `breed` attributes when an object is created. We also define a `bark` method that prints a message.

To create an object (an instance) of the `Dog` class, you call the class like a function:

```python
my_dog = Dog("Buddy", "Labrador")
```

Now, `my_dog` is an object of the `Dog` class with the `name` attribute set to "Buddy" and the `breed` attribute set to "Labrador". You can access the attributes and call the methods of an object using dot notation:

```python
print(my_dog.name) # Output: Buddy
my_dog.bark() # Output: Buddy says: Woof!
```

Inheritance and Polymorphism

Inheritance is a mechanism that allows a new class (a subclass or derived class) to inherit attributes and methods from an existing class (a superclass or base class). This promotes code reuse and enables the creation of specialized versions of classes.

To create a subclass in Python, you define a new class that inherits from the superclass:

```
class GoldenRetriever(Dog):
def fetch(self):
print(f"{self.name} is fetching the stick!")
```

In this example, the `GoldenRetriever` class is a subclass of the `Dog` class. It inherits the `name` and `breed` attributes, as well as the `bark` method, from the `Dog` class. Additionally, it defines a new `fetch` method specific to the `GoldenRetriever` class.

Polymorphism is the ability of objects of different classes to be treated as objects of a common superclass. This allows for flexibility and extensibility in your code. In Python, polymorphism is achieved through method overriding, where a subclass provides its own implementation of a method that is already defined in the superclass.

```
class Bulldog(Dog):
def bark(self):
print(f"{self.name} says: Woof woof!")
my_bulldog = Bulldog("Buster", "Bulldog")
my_bulldog.bark() # Output: Buster says: Woof woof!
```

In this example, the `Bulldog` class overrides the `bark` method from the `Dog` class with its own implementation. When you call the `bark` method on an instance of the `Bulldog` class, the overridden version of the method is executed.

Magic Methods (Dunder Methods)

In Python, magic methods (also known as dunder methods) are special methods that allow you to define how objects of a class behave in specific situations. They are surrounded by double underscores, such as `__init__` and `__str__`.

Here are some common magic methods:

- `__init__(self, ...)`: This method is called when an object is created and is used to initialize the object's attributes.

- `__str__(self)`: This method is called when you try to convert an object to a string representation using `str(obj)` or by printing the object directly.

- `__len__(self)`: This method is called when you use the `len()` function on an object to get its length.

- `__add__(self, other)`: This method is called when you use the `+` operator to add two objects together.

- `__iter__(self)`: This method is called when you iterate over an object using a `for` loop or other iteration constructs.

Here's an example that demonstrates the use of the `__str__` and `__len__` magic methods:

```python
class Kennel:
    def __init__(self):
        self.dogs = []
    def add_dog(self, dog):
        self.dogs.append(dog)
    def __str__(self):
        return f"Kennel with {len(self.dogs)} dogs"
    def __len__(self):
        return len(self.dogs)
```

```python
my_kennel = Kennel()
my_kennel.add_dog(Dog("Buddy", "Labrador"))
my_kennel.add_dog(Dog("Lola", "Poodle"))
print(my_kennel) # Output: Kennel with 2 dogs
print(len(my_kennel)) # Output: 2
```

In this example, the `Kennel` class has a `__str__` method that returns a string representation of the object, and a `__len__` method that returns the number of dogs in the kennel. When you print an instance of the `Kennel` class or use the `len()` function on it, these magic methods are automatically called.

Magic methods provide a way to define how objects of a class should behave in specific situations, enabling you to create more intuitive and Pythonic classes. They are an essential part of object-oriented programming in Python and allow you to create objects that seamlessly integrate with Python's built-in functions and operators.

Chapter 8: Functional Programming

Introduction

Functional programming is a programming paradigm that emphasizes the use of pure functions, immutable data, and the avoidance of side effects. It is a declarative style of programming where the focus is on describing what needs to be done, rather than how it should be done. Functional programming differs from procedural and object-oriented programming in several ways:

- **Procedural Programming**: This paradigm is centered around step-by-step instructions and focuses on how to perform a task. It involves breaking down a problem into a series of smaller steps, each with its own set of instructions.
- **Object-Oriented Programming (OOP)**: This paradigm is based on the concept of objects, which are instances of classes. OOP focuses on combining data and behavior into reusable units called objects, promoting code reusability, modularity, and encapsulation.
- **Functional Programming**: This paradigm is centered around pure functions, which are functions that always return the same output for a given input and have no side effects (i.e., they do not modify any external state). Functional programming emphasizes immutable data and treats functions as first-class citizens, meaning they can be assigned to variables, passed as arguments to other functions, and returned from functions.

The benefits of functional programming include:

- **Simplicity**: Pure functions are easier to reason about and test because they have no side effects and always produce the same output for a given input.

- **Predictability**: Functional code is more predictable and easier to debug because it avoids mutable state and side effects.
- **Parallelization**: Functional code is easier to parallelize because it avoids shared mutable state, which can lead to race conditions and other concurrency issues.
- **Modularity**: Functional programming promotes the creation of small, reusable functions that can be easily composed to solve complex problems.

Python supports functional programming concepts, making it a multi-paradigm language that allows you to combine functional programming with procedural and object-oriented programming.

First-Class Functions

In programming, first-class citizens are entities that can be treated like any other value. In Python, functions are first-class citizens, which means they can be assigned to variables, stored in collections (e.g., lists, dictionaries), and passed as arguments to other functions.

Here's an example of assigning a function to a variable:

```python
def greet(name):
    return f"Hello, {name}!"
greeting_func = greet
print(greeting_func("Alice")) # Output: Hello, Alice!
```

In this example, the greet function is assigned to the greeting_func variable, and we can call it like any other function.

Functions can also be passed as arguments to other functions, which are known as higher-order functions. Higher-order functions are functions that take one or more functions as arguments or return a function as a result.

```python
def apply_twice(func, value):
    return func(func(value))
def square(x):
    return x * x
print(apply_twice(square, 3)) # Output: 81
```

In this example, the apply_twice function is a higher-order function that takes another function (func) and a value (value) as arguments. It then applies the func function twice to the value and returns the result.

Map, Filter, and Reduce

Pure functions are functions that have no side effects and always return
the same output for a given input. In Python, the built-in map, filter,
and reduce functions are pure functions that operate on iterables (e.g.,
lists, tuples, strings) and are often used in functional programming.

- **map(func, iterable)**: The map function applies a given
  function (func) to each element of an iterable and returns a
  new iterable with the transformed elements.

```python
numbers = [1, 2, 3, 4, 5]
squared_numbers = list(map(lambda x: x ** 2, numbers))
print(squared_numbers) # Output: [1, 4, 9, 16, 25]
```

In this example, the map function applies a lambda function
(lambda x: x ** 2) to each element of the numbers list, creating a new
list with the squared values.

- **filter(func, iterable)**: The filter function creates a new
  iterable with elements from the original iterable for which
  the given function (func) returns True.

```python
numbers = [1, 2, 3, 4, 5, 6, 7, 8, 9, 10]
even_numbers = list(filter(lambda x: x % 2 == 0, numbers))
print(even_numbers) # Output: [2, 4, 6, 8, 10]
```

In this example, the filter function creates a new list containing
only the even numbers from the numbers list, using a lambda function
(lambda x: x % 2 == 0) to check if each element is even.

- **reduce(func, iterable, initializer)**: The reduce function applies a given function (func) of two arguments cumulatively to the elements of an iterable, from left to right, to reduce the iterable to a single value. If an initializer is provided, it is used as the initial value for the reduction.

```
from functools import reduce
numbers = [1, 2, 3, 4, 5]
sum_of_numbers = reduce(lambda x, y: x + y, numbers)
print(sum_of_numbers) # Output: 15
```

In this example, the reduce function is used to sum up all the elements of the numbers list, using a lambda function (lambda x, y: x + y) that adds two elements together. Since no initializer is provided, the first two elements of the list are used as the initial values for the reduction.

These functions (map, filter, and reduce) are often used in conjunction with lambda functions to create concise and expressive functional code.

Closures and Decorators

Closures

A closure is a function object that has access to variables in the outer (enclosing) function's scope, even after the outer function has finished executing. Closures are created when a nested function is defined within another function and the nested function references variables from the enclosing scope.

```python
def outer_func(x):
    y = 4 # Free variable
    def inner_func(z):
        return x + y + z # Closure captures x and y
    return inner_func
closure = outer_func(2)
print(closure(3)) # Output: 9
```

In this example, the inner_func is a closure because it captures and has access to the x and y variables from the outer_func scope, even after outer_func has finished executing. When we call closure(3), the inner_func can still access the values of x (2) and y (4) from the enclosing scope, and it adds them to the argument z (3), resulting in the output of 9.

Closures are useful for creating private variables and functions, implementing decorators, and creating function factories.

Decorators

In Python, a decorator is a function that takes another function as an argument, adds some functionality to it, and returns a new function. Decorators provide a way to modify or extend the behavior of functions without changing their source code directly.

```python
def uppercase(func):
def wrapper(*args, **kwargs):
result = func(*args, **kwargs)
return result.upper()
return wrapper
@uppercase
def greet(name):
return f"Hello, {name}!"
print(greet("Alice")) # Output: HELLO, ALICE!
```

In this example, the uppercase decorator takes a function func as an argument and returns a new function wrapper. The wrapper function calls the original func with the provided arguments (*args and **kwargs), and then it applies the .upper() method to the result before returning it.

The @uppercase syntax is a shorthand way of applying the uppercase decorator to the greet function. It's equivalent to writing greet = uppercase(greet).

Decorators can be used for various purposes, such as memoization (caching function results), logging, timing functions, authentication, and more. They provide a way to add functionality to functions without modifying their source code, promoting code reusability and separation of concerns.

```python
import time
def timer(func):
def wrapper(*args, **kwargs):
start_time = time.time()
```

```python
    result = func(*args, **kwargs)
    end_time = time.time()
    print(f"Function '{func.__name__}' took {end_time - start_time:.6f} seconds.")
    return result
  return wrapper
@timer
def slow_function(n):
  result = 0
  for i in range(n):
    result += i
  return result
slow_function(10000000)
# Output: Function 'slow_function' took 0.123456 seconds.
```

In this example, the timer decorator is used to measure the execution time of the slow_function. When slow_function is called, the timer decorator wraps it with the wrapper function, which records the start and end times and prints the elapsed time.

Functional programming in Python provides powerful tools and techniques for writing concise, expressive, and maintainable code. By leveraging first-class functions, pure functions like map, filter, and reduce, as well as closures and decorators, you can create modular and reusable code that is easier to reason about, test, and parallelize. While Python supports multiple programming paradigms, incorporating functional programming principles can lead to more robust, scalable, and elegant solutions.

Chapter 9: Concurrency and Multithreading

Introduction

Concurrency and multithreading are concepts that allow you to take advantage of modern computer hardware by executing multiple tasks simultaneously. This can lead to improved performance, responsiveness, and resource utilization in your applications.

Concurrency refers to the ability of a program to make progress on multiple tasks simultaneously. This can be achieved through various techniques, such as multithreading, multiprocessing, or asynchronous programming.

Multithreading is a form of concurrency where a single process can have multiple threads of execution running concurrently. Each thread runs independently and can execute different parts of the program's code simultaneously, sharing the same memory space.

Concurrency and multithreading are useful in scenarios where you have tasks that can be executed independently or in parallel, such as handling multiple network requests, performing CPU-bound calculations, or updating a graphical user interface (GUI) while performing other operations.

2. Threading and Multiprocessing

In Python, you can achieve concurrency through threading and multiprocessing. The main difference between these two approaches lies in how they utilize system resources and share data.

Threading

Python provides the `threading` module for creating and managing threads. Threads in Python are lightweight and can be created and managed with relatively low overhead. However, due to the Global Interpreter Lock (GIL) in CPython (the standard Python implementation), only one thread can execute Python bytecode at a time. This means that while threads can be useful for I/O-bound tasks, such as network operations or file I/O, they may not provide significant performance benefits for CPU-bound tasks.

Here's an example of creating and starting a new thread:

```python
import threading
def worker():
print("Worker thread running...")
# Perform some task
thread = threading.Thread(target=worker)
thread.start()
```

Multiprocessing

The `multiprocessing` module in Python allows you to create and manage separate processes, each with its own memory space and GIL. This approach can be more effective for CPU-bound tasks, as each process can run on a separate CPU core or processor, allowing for true parallelism.

Here's an example of creating and starting a new process:

```python
import multiprocessing
def worker():
print("Worker process running...")
# Perform some task
process = multiprocessing.Process(target=worker)
process.start()
```

While multiprocessing can offer better performance for CPU-bound tasks, it comes with additional overhead due to the separate memory spaces and inter-process communication requirements.

Synchronization and Locks

When working with concurrent programs, synchronization is crucial to prevent race conditions and ensure data integrity. A race condition occurs when two or more threads or processes access shared data concurrently, and the final result depends on the relative timing of their execution.

Locks are a synchronization mechanism used to control access to shared resources. When a thread or process acquires a lock, it has exclusive access to the protected resource, preventing other threads or processes from accessing it until the lock is released.

Python provides several types of locks, including `Lock`, `RLock` (reentrant lock), and `Semaphore`. Here's an example of using a `Lock` to protect a shared counter:

```python
import threading
counter = 0
lock = threading.Lock()
def increment_counter():
global counter
for _ in range(100000):
with lock:
counter += 1
threads = []
for _ in range(5):
thread = threading.Thread(target=increment_counter)
threads.append(thread)
thread.start()
for thread in threads:
thread.join()
print(f"Final counter value: {counter}")
```

In this example, the `lock` is used to ensure that only one thread can access and modify the `counter` variable at a time, preventing race conditions and ensuring the final counter value is accurate.

Asynchronous Programming (asyncio)

Asynchronous programming is a different approach to concurrency that allows a program to run multiple tasks concurrently without the need for separate threads or processes. Instead of blocking while waiting for I/O operations to complete, asynchronous code allows the program to continue executing other tasks and handles the I/O operations when they are ready.

Python's `asyncio` module provides a framework for writing asynchronous code using the `async` and `await` keywords. Asynchronous programming can be particularly useful for I/O-bound tasks, such as network operations, file I/O, and database interactions, where the program would typically spend a significant amount of time waiting for responses.

Here's an example of using `asyncio` to perform concurrent network requests:

```python
import asyncio
import aiohttp
async def fetch_data(url):
async with aiohttp.ClientSession() as session:
async with session.get(url) as response:
data = await response.text()
print(f"Received data from {url}: {data}")
async def main():
urls = [
"https://example.com/data1",
"https://example.com/data2",
"https://example.com/data3",
]
tasks = []
for url in urls:
tasks.append(asyncio.create_task(fetch_data(url)))
```

```
await asyncio.gather(*tasks)
asyncio.run(main())
```

In this example, the `fetch_data` coroutine function performs an asynchronous HTTP request using the `aiohttp` library. The `main` coroutine creates multiple tasks by calling `fetch_data` for each URL and uses `asyncio.gather` to wait for all tasks to complete.

Asynchronous programming with `asyncio` can offer significant performance benefits for I/O-bound applications, as it allows the program to effectively utilize system resources by avoiding blocking operations and enabling concurrent execution of multiple tasks.

Concurrency and multithreading are powerful concepts that enable you to write efficient and responsive applications in Python. Whether you choose to use threading, multiprocessing, or asynchronous programming with `asyncio`, understanding the principles of concurrency and the tools available in Python can help you leverage the full potential of modern hardware and improve the overall performance and responsiveness of your applications.

Chapter 10: Best Practices and Tips

Introduction to Best Practices and Tips

Writing good code is not just about making it work; it's also about writing code that is readable, maintainable, and efficient. Following best practices and tips in Python programming can help you write better code, save time, and make your life easier as a developer. These practices and tips are guidelines that have been developed by experienced programmers over time and have proven to be effective in producing high-quality code.

Code Readability and PEP 8

Code readability is crucial for collaboration, maintainability, and future understanding of your own code. The Python community has adopted a set of guidelines called PEP 8 (Python Enhancement Proposal 8) to promote a consistent coding style across Python projects.

PEP 8 covers various aspects of code formatting, such as:

- Indentation: Use 4 spaces per indentation level (no tabs).

- Line length: Keep lines within 79 characters, if possible.

- Blank lines: Use blank lines to separate logical sections of code.

- Naming conventions: Use descriptive names for variables, functions, and classes (e.g., `my_variable`, `function_name`, `ClassName`).

- Whitespace: Use whitespace to improve readability (e.g., spaces around operators, after commas, etc.).

Following PEP 8 guidelines can make your code more readable and consistent with the broader Python community, which can be beneficial when collaborating with other developers or working on open-source projects.

Effective Use of Comments

Comments are an essential part of writing readable and maintainable code. They help explain the purpose, logic, and reasoning behind your code, making it easier for others (and your future self) to understand and modify it.

However, comments should be used judiciously and not as a substitute for writing clear and self-documenting code. Here are some tips for effective commenting:

- Explain the "why" rather than the "what": Your code should be self-explanatory for the "what," but comments can clarify the reasoning behind your choices.

- Use docstrings: Python's docstrings (triple-quoted strings at the beginning of a module, class, or function) provide a standardized way to document code.

- Keep comments up-to-date: As your code evolves, ensure that your comments remain relevant and accurate.

- Avoid redundant comments: Don't repeat what the code already explains clearly.

- Use meaningful variable and function names: Well-named identifiers can often make comments unnecessary.

Naming Conventions in Python

Python has established naming conventions for different types of identifiers (variables, functions, classes, modules, etc.). Following these conventions can improve code readability and consistency:

- Variables: Use lowercase with words separated by underscores (`my_variable`).

- Functions: Use lowercase with words separated by underscores (`my_function`).

- Classes: Use CapitalizedWords (also known as UpperCamelCase) (`MyClass`).

- Modules: Use lowercase with words separated by underscores (`my_module.py`).

- Constants: Use all uppercase with words separated by underscores (`MY_CONSTANT`).

Adhering to these conventions makes your code more consistent with the Python community and easier for other developers to understand.

Error Handling and Exceptions

Proper error handling is essential for writing robust and reliable code. Python provides an exception handling mechanism using the `try`/`except` blocks, which allow you to catch and handle exceptions gracefully.

```
try:
result = x / y
except ZeroDivisionError:
print("Error: Division by zero")
except Exception as e:
print(f"An error occurred: {e}")
else:
print(f"Result: {result}")
finally:
print("This block always runs")
```

In this example, the code attempts to divide `x` by `y`. If a `ZeroDivisionError` occurs, a specific message is printed. If any other exception occurs, a generic error message is printed. The `else` block executes if no exceptions are raised, and the `finally` block always runs, regardless of whether an exception was raised or not.

Proper error handling not only makes your code more robust but also provides better user experiences and easier debugging.

Efficient Use of Data Structures

Python provides a variety of built-in data structures, such as lists, dictionaries, sets, and tuples. Choosing the right data structure for your task can significantly impact the efficiency and performance of your code.

For example, if you need to frequently check for the existence of elements, a set is more efficient than a list. If you need to associate keys with values, a dictionary is the appropriate choice. If you need an ordered sequence of elements, a list is suitable.

Understanding the strengths and weaknesses of each data structure can help you write more efficient and optimized code.

Optimizing Code Performance

While Python is generally known for its simplicity and readability, there are times when you may need to optimize your code for better performance. Here are some tips for optimizing code performance:

- Use built-in functions and modules: Python's built-in functions and modules are typically implemented in C and are highly optimized for performance.

- Avoid unnecessary computations: Identify and eliminate unnecessary computations or redundant operations in your code.

- Use generators and iterators: Generators and iterators can be more memory-efficient than creating large lists or other data structures.

- Utilize caching: If your code performs expensive computations or fetches data from external sources, consider caching the results to avoid redundant work.

- Profile your code: Use profiling tools to identify performance bottlenecks in your code and focus your optimization efforts on those areas.

Remember that premature optimization can often lead to complex and harder-to-maintain code. Always prioritize readability and maintainability, and only optimize when necessary and after profiling your code.

Writing Clean and Maintainable Code

Writing clean and maintainable code is essential for long-term project success and collaboration. Here are some strategies to keep your code clean and maintainable:

- Follow the SOLID principles: The SOLID principles (Single Responsibility, Open/Closed, Liskov Substitution, Interface Segregation, and Dependency Inversion) provide guidelines for writing modular and extensible code.

- Keep functions and classes small: Small, focused functions and classes are easier to understand, maintain, and test.

- Avoid code duplication: Duplicated code can lead to maintenance nightmares. Use functions, modules, or inheritance to eliminate code duplication.

- Write self-documenting code: Use meaningful variable and function names, and write code that is easy to understand without excessive comments.

- Follow a consistent coding style: Adhere to a consistent coding style, such as PEP 8, to improve readability and maintainability.

By following these strategies, you can create code that is easier to understand, modify, and extend, both for yourself and for other developers who may work on the project.

Testing and Debugging Techniques

Testing and debugging are essential parts of the software development process. Python provides several tools and techniques to help you write and debug your code effectively:

- Unit testing: Use Python's built-in `unittest` module or third-party testing frameworks like `pytest` to write and run unit tests for your code.

- Debugging with `pdb`: Python's built-in `pdb` module is a powerful debugger that allows you to step through your code, set breakpoints, and inspect variables.

- Logging: The `logging` module in Python provides a flexible and configurable way to log messages, warnings, and errors, which can be invaluable for debugging and troubleshooting.

- Linting: Use linters like `pylint` or `flake8` to check your code for compliance with Python coding standards and best practices, as well as potential errors or issues.

- Profiling: Use profiling tools like `cProfile` or third-party tools like `line_profiler` to identify performance bottlenecks in your code.

Regular testing and effective debugging techniques can help you catch and fix issues early, improve code quality, and increase confidence in your application.

Continuous Learning and Improvement

Programming is a constantly evolving field, and continuous learning and improvement are essential for staying up-to-date and becoming a better programmer. Here are some tips for continuous learning and improvement:

- Read code written by others: Reading and understanding code written by experienced developers can help you learn new techniques and best practices.

- Attend conferences and meetups: Conferences and meetups provide excellent opportunities to learn from experts, network with other developers, and stay updated on the latest trends and technologies.

- Contribute to open-source projects: Contributing to open-source projects can expose you to different coding styles, practices, and workflows, while also allowing you to give back to the community.

- Learn from online resources: Take advantage of online resources such as tutorials, blogs, and coding challenges to continually expand your knowledge and skills.

- Experiment and practice: The more you experiment and practice, the better you'll become at programming. Set aside time to work on personal projects or try out new technologies.

Chapter 11: Advanced Python Features

Python is a powerful and flexible programming language, and while its simplicity allows beginners to pick it up quickly, it also offers a range of advanced features that are valuable for experienced programmers. These advanced features can help you write more efficient, concise, and maintainable code.

Understanding Iterators and Generators

An iterator in Python is an object that can be iterated (looped) upon. An object which will return data, one element at a time. This is a very powerful tool in Python as it allows you to handle large amounts of data efficiently, which is often required in data science or machine learning tasks.

Creating Your Own Iterator

Creating an iterator in Python requires implementing two methods in your iterator class, __iter__ and __next__. The __iter__ method returns the iterator object itself, while the __next__ method returns the next value from the iterator. Here's an example of a simple iterator:

```python
class MyIterator:
def __init__(self, max_val):
self.max_val = max_val
self.curr_val = 0
def __iter__(self):
return self
def __next__(self):
if self.curr_val <= self.max_val:
result = self.curr_val
self.curr_val += 1
return result
else:
raise StopIteration
```

Introduction to Generators

Generators are a type of iterable, like lists or tuples. Unlike lists, they don't allow indexing with arbitrary indices, but they can still be iterated through with for loops. They are created using functions and the yield statement.

Creating Your Own Generator

Creating a generator in Python is as simple as defining a normal function, but with the yield statement instead of return. The yield statement pauses the function and saves the local state so that it can be resumed right where it left off when next values are needed. Here's an example of a simple generator:

```
def my_generator(max_val):
num = 0
while num <= max_val:
yield num
num += 1
```

Comparing Iterators and Generators

While both iterators and generators allow you to iterate over a sequence of values, the key difference is that generators use the yield keyword, which makes them much easier to implement than a class-based iterator. However, generators can only be iterated over once, while iterators can be used multiple times.

Decorators and Context Managers

Decorators allow us to wrap another function in order to extend the behavior of the wrapped function, without permanently modifying it. In Python, decorators are implemented as functions or classes that take a function (or class) as an input and return a function (or class) as an output.

Creating Your Own Decorator

Creating a decorator involves defining a function that takes a function as an argument and returns a new function that includes the old function inside the closure.

```python
def my_decorator(func):
def wrapper():
print("Before function call")
func()
print("After function call")
return wrapper
@my_decorator
def say_hello():
print("Hello!")
say_hello()
```

Introduction to Context Managers

Context managers in Python are used to properly manage resources so that we can specify exactly what we want to set up and tear down when working with them.

Creating Your Own Context Manager

Creating a context manager in Python involves defining a class with __enter__ and __exit__ methods.

```
class MyContextManager:
def __enter__(self):
print("Entering the block")
return self
def __exit__(self, type, value, traceback):
print("Exiting the block")
with MyContextManager() as x:
print("Inside the block")
```

Practical Applications of Decorators and Context Managers

Decorators are widely used in Python development for a variety of tasks, including logging, timing functions, enforcing access control and authentication, and more. Context managers are typically used for managing resources that need explicit setup or teardown steps, such as files, network connections, and locks.

Working with Metaclasses

Metaclasses are the 'classes' of classes, meaning they control the creation and behavior of classes just like classes control the creation and behavior of objects. The type is the built-in metaclass in Python, but you can create your own metaclasses.

Creating Your Own Metaclass

Creating a metaclass in Python involves defining a class that inherits from type. A metaclass can override the __new__ or __init__ methods to customize class creation.

```python
class MyMeta(type):
def __new__(cls, name, bases, dct):
print("Creating class", name)
return super().__new__(cls, name, bases, dct)
def __init__(cls, name, bases, dct):
print("Initializing class", name)
super().__init__(name, bases, dct)
class MyClass(metaclass=MyMeta):
pass
```

Practical Applications of Metaclasses

Metaclasses can be used for a variety of advanced tasks, such as logging class creation, enforcing coding standards, freezing class attributes, and more. However, they should be used sparingly due to their complexity.

Understanding the Metaclass Hook

Python provides a hook at the end of class statement - the __init_subclass__ method. This method is called on the base class whenever a subclass is created. This can be used to manage subclasses and perform certain tasks whenever a subclass is created.

```python
class MyBaseClass:
def __init_subclass__(cls, **kwargs):
print(f"Creating subclass {cls} with attributes {kwargs}")
class MySubClass(MyBaseClass, attribute1="value1", attribute2="value2"):
    pass
```

Memory Management and Garbage Collection

Memory management in Python involves a private heap containing all Python objects and data structures. The management of this private heap is ensured internally by the Python memory manager. The allocation of heap space for Python objects is done by Python's memory manager, so the programmer does not have access to the private heap.

Python's Memory Manager

The core API of Python provides some tools for the programmer to code reliable and more robust programs. Python's memory manager handles the allocation of Python memory from the private heap space. While programming, you don't need to worry about new memory allocation or freeing up memory space when creating new objects in Python. Python's memory manager does it all for you.

```python
# Example of memory management in Python
import sys
print("Total memory: ", sys.total_memory_size())
a = [1, 2, 3]
print("Memory usage after creating a list: ", sys.get_memory_usage())
```

Garbage Collection in Python

Garbage Collection (GC) in Python works by counting the number of references to an object. When references to an object are removed, the reference count for an object is decremented. When the reference count becomes zero, the object is deallocated, meaning the space for the object in the heap is cleared.

```python
# Example of garbage collection in Python
import gc
print("Garbage collection is ", gc.is_enabled())
gc.disable()
print("Garbage collection is ", gc.is_enabled())
gc.enable()
print("Garbage collection is ", gc.is_enabled())
```

The gc Module

Python also has a built-in garbage collector, which recycles all the unused memory and frees the memory and makes it available to the heap space. The gc module provides the ability to disable the collector, tune the collection frequency, and set debugging options.

```
# Example of using the gc module
import gc
gc.collect() # runs a manual garbage collection
```

Reference Counting

Python uses a technique called reference counting to keep track of the number of references to an object. An object's reference count increases when it's assigned a new name or placed in a container (list, tuple, or dictionary). The object's reference count decreases when it's deleted with del, its reference is reassigned, or its reference goes out of scope. When an object's reference count reaches zero, Python collects it automatically.

```python
# Example of reference counting
import sys
class MyObject:
def __init__(self):
print("Creating a new object")
self.counter = 0
def __del__(self):
print("Deleting the object")
my_object = MyObject()
my_object_id = id(my_object)
print("Reference count: ", sys.getrefcount(my_object))
my_object = None
print("Reference count: ", sys.getrefcount(my_object))
```

Practical Implications of Memory Management

Understanding Python's memory management can help you write more efficient and performant code. For example, knowing how Python's GC works can help you manage memory in your applications better, especially for high-load applications.

Object Model

Python is an object-oriented programming language, and its object model allows for a high degree of flexibility and power. In Python, everything is an object, including numbers, strings, functions, classes, instances, and even types themselves.

```
print(type(123)) # <class 'int'>
print(type("hello")) # <class 'str'>
print(type(len)) # <class 'builtin_function_or_method'>
```

Understanding Python Objects

In Python, an object is a collection of data and instructions held in computer memory that consists of an identity, a type, and a value. The identity never changes once an object has been created; you can think of it as the object's address in memory. The type of an object determines what kind of object it is; for example, whether it is a number, a string, a list, etc. The value of some objects can change. Objects whose value can change are said to be mutable; objects whose value is unchangeable once they are created are called immutable.

    x = [1, 2, 3] # mutable
    y = (1, 2, 3) # immutable

Python's Data Model

Python's data model allows you to define how your objects behave in various situations - for example, when they're included in a for loop, or when they're printed. You can define methods on your objects like __iter__, __len__, or __str__, and Python will call these methods when your objects are used in situations calling for these methods.

```python
class MyClass:
def __init__(self, length):
self.length = length
def __len__(self):
return self.length
def __str__(self):
return f"MyClass(length={self.length})"
obj = MyClass(5)
print(len(obj)) # 5
print(obj) # MyClass(length=5)
```

Understanding Classes and Instances

In Python, a class is a code template for creating objects. Objects have member variables and have behavior associated with them. An object is created using the constructor of the class. This object will then be called the instance of the class.

```python
class MyClass:
def __init__(self, value):
self.value = value
instance = MyClass(5)
print(instance.value) # 5
```

Understanding Python's Method Resolution Order (MRO)

Python's MRO is the order in which the base classes are searched when executing a method. First, the method or attribute is searched within the class itself. Then it follows the order in the base classes from left to right. This is also known as a linearization of the class and the set of rules are called C3 Linearization or just C3.

```python
class A:
pass
class B(A):
pass
class C(A):
pass
class D(B, C):
pass
print(D.mro()) # [<class '__main__.D'>, <class '__main__.B'>,
<class '__main__.C'>, <class '__main__.A'>, <class 'object'>]
```

Practical Implications of Python's Object Model

Understanding Python's object model can help you write more efficient and cleaner code. It allows you to understand how Python's features work under the hood, and can help you make better design decisions when creating your own objects and classes.

Advanced Exception Handling

Exception handling in Python involves using try, except, else, and finally blocks to catch and handle exceptions. Python raises an exception whenever it encounters an error from which it cannot recover.

```python
try:
# code that may raise an exception
x = 1 / 0
except ZeroDivisionError:
# code that handles the exception
print("You can't divide by zero!")
```

Understanding Python's Exception Hierarchy

All exceptions in Python are derived from the BaseException class. The direct subclasses of BaseException are SystemExit, KeyboardInterrupt, GeneratorExit, and Exception. Most of the built-in exceptions are derived from the Exception class.

Creating Your Own Exceptions

You can create your own exceptions in Python by creating a new class that inherits from the Exception class or one of its subclasses.

```python
class MyException(Exception):
pass
try:
raise MyException("This is a custom exception")
except MyException as e:
print(e)
```

Using the else and finally Clauses

The else clause in a try/except block will be executed if no exceptions were raised. The finally clause will be executed no matter what, and is generally used for cleanup code.

```python
try:
print("Hello, world!")
except Exception:
print("An error occurred")
else:
print("No errors occurred")
finally:
print("This is the end")
```

Practical Implications of Advanced Exception Handling

Understanding advanced exception handling can help you write more robust code that can handle unexpected situations gracefully. It allows you to control the flow of your program and provide useful error messages to your users.

Working with Python's Abstract Base Classes

In Python, Abstract Base Classes (ABCs) are a way to define interfaces that a class must implement. They provide a way to define a common set of methods that a class must have, without providing an implementation for those methods. This allows for a more robust and maintainable codebase.

Creating an Abstract Base Class

To create an abstract base class, you can use the abc module from the standard library. Here's an example of an abstract base class for a shape:

```python
import abc
class Shape(metaclass=abc.ABCMeta):
@abc.abstractmethod
def area(self):
pass
@abc.abstractmethod
def perimeter(self):
pass
```

In this example, the Shape class has two abstract methods, area and perimeter, that must be implemented by any class that inherits from Shape.

Implementing an Abstract Base Class

Here's an example of a class that inherits from Shape and implements the abstract methods:

```python
class Rectangle(Shape):
def __init__(self, width, height):
self.width = width
self.height = height
def area(self):
return self.width * self.height
def perimeter(self):
return 2 * (self.width + self.height)
```

In this example, the Rectangle class has a constructor that takes in the width and height of the rectangle, and it implements the area and perimeter methods.

Checking if a Class Implements an Abstract Base Class

You can use the abc module to check if a class implements an abstract base class. Here's an example:

```python
from abc import ABC, abstractmethod
class Shape(ABC):
@abstractmethod
def area(self):
pass
@abstractmethod
def perimeter(self):
pass
class Rectangle(Shape):
def __init__(self, width, height):
self.width = width
self.height = height
def area(self):
return self.width * self.height
def perimeter(self):
return 2 * (self.width + self.height)
# Check if Rectangle implements Shape
print(issubclass(Rectangle, Shape)) # Output: True
```

Practical Implications of Abstract Base Classes

Using abstract base classes can help ensure that a class implements a certain set of methods, which can make your code more robust and maintainable. It can also help with code organization and readability, as it provides a clear interface for a class to implement. Additionally, it can help with testing, as you can create test cases that check if a class implements an abstract base class.

Asynchronous Programming and Coroutines

Asynchronous programming is a way of writing code that allows for non-blocking execution of tasks. This means that while one task is waiting for an operation to complete (such as a network request), other tasks can continue to run. This can lead to significant performance improvements in I/O bound applications.

Asynchronous Programming

Asynchronous programming in Python is made possible through the use of coroutines. A coroutine is a special type of function that can suspend its execution and pass control to another coroutine. This allows for the non-blocking execution of tasks.

Coroutines

Here's an example of a coroutine:

```python
import asyncio
async def main():
print("Hello")
await asyncio.sleep(1)
print("World")
asyncio.run(main())
```

In this example, the main function is a coroutine. The async keyword is used to define a coroutine. The await keyword is used to suspend the execution of the coroutine and pass control to another coroutine. In this case, the asyncio.sleep function is called with a delay of 1 second. This allows other tasks to run while the current task is waiting for the delay to complete.

Asynchronous Functions

Asynchronous functions are functions that can be called from a coroutine. They are defined using the async def syntax. Here's an example:

```python
import asyncio
async def get_data(url):
async with aiohttp.ClientSession() as session:
async with session.get(url) as response:
data = await response.text()
return data
async def main():
url = "https://www.example.com"
data = await get_data(url)
print(data)
asyncio.run(main())
```

In this example, the get_data function is an asynchronous function. It uses the aiohttp library to make a network request. The async with statement is used to create a new session and request. The await keyword is used to suspend the execution of the coroutine and pass control to another coroutine while the network request is being made.

Practical Implications of Asynchronous Programming

Asynchronous programming can lead to significant performance improvements in I/O bound applications. It allows for the non-blocking execution of tasks, which can lead to better use of system resources. Additionally, it can make your code more readable and maintainable, as it separates the concerns of I/O bound tasks and CPU bound tasks.

It's important to note that asynchronous programming is not always the best solution. It adds complexity to your code and can make it harder to debug. It's best used in situations where you have a lot of I/O bound tasks, such as network requests or file I/O.

Exploring Python's C API

The Python C API is a set of functions and types that allow you to write C code that interacts with Python. It provides a way to extend and embed the Python interpreter.

Extending Python

The Python C API can be used to extend the functionality of Python by writing C code that can be imported as a Python module. This allows you to write high-performance code in C and make it available to Python.

Here's an example of a C file that defines a function that can be imported as a Python module:

```c
#include <Python.h>
double add(double a, double b) {
return a + b;
}
static PyMethodDef methods[] = {
{"add", (PyCFunction)add, METH_VARARGS, "Adds two numbers."},
{NULL, NULL, 0, NULL}
};
static struct PyModuleDef module = {
PyModuleDef_HEAD_INIT,
"mymodule",
"My module documentation.",
-1,
methods
};
PyMODINIT_FUNC PyInit_mymodule(void) {
return PyModule_Create(&module);
}
```

In this example, the add function is defined in C and can be imported as a Python function. The methods array defines the functions that will be available in the Python module. The PyMODINIT_FUNC macro is used to define the initialization function for the module.

Embedding Python

The Python C API can also be used to embed the Python interpreter in a C application. This allows you to use Python scripts and modules in a C application.

Here's an example of a C file that embeds the Python interpreter:

```c
#include <Python.h>
int main(int argc, char *argv[]) {
Py_Initialize();
PyRun_SimpleString("import sys");
PyRun_SimpleString("print(sys.path)");
Py_Finalize();
return 0;
}
```

In this example, the Python interpreter is initialized and the sys module is imported. The PyRun_SimpleString function is used to execute a Python script.

Practical Implications of the Python C API

The Python C API provides a powerful way to extend and embed the Python interpreter. It allows you to write high-performance code in C and make it available to Python. Additionally, it allows you to use Python scripts and modules in a C application.

It's important to note that using the Python C API adds complexity to your code and can make it harder to maintain. It's best used in situations where you need to write high-performance code or use Python scripts and modules in a C application.